Table Of Contents

Chapter 1: The Rise of AI Supermodels

The Evolution of Modeling in the Digital Age

The digital age has revolutionized the way we perceive and interact with models, introducing a dynamic shift that has redefined beauty standards and marketing strategies. Gone are the days when modeling was solely confined to human figures walking down runways or gracing magazine covers. With the advent of advanced artificial intelligence technologies, we now have the emergence of AI-generated supermodels, who are not only captivating audiences but also driving unprecedented profitability in the fashion and advertising industries. This evolution has opened up a new frontier for aspiring Insta-Millionaires, allowing them to tap into a market that is both innovative and lucrative.

AI-generated models present a unique opportunity for brands and influencers alike. They can be meticulously designed to embody diverse beauty ideals, making them appealing to a wider audience. This digital flexibility allows for the creation of supermodels that resonate with various demographics, thus increasing engagement and brand loyalty. Brands can now launch targeted marketing campaigns featuring these virtual personas, ensuring that they connect with consumers on a personal level, which is essential in today's fast-paced social media landscape. The result? A stunningly effective way to captivate audiences and drive significant sales.

Moreover, the cost-effectiveness of utilizing AI-generated models cannot be overstated. Traditional modeling entails expenses like agency fees, travel costs, and extensive production budgets. In contrast, virtual models can be created and maintained with a fraction of these costs. This allows brands to allocate resources more strategically, investing in innovative marketing tactics that can further enhance their reach and profitability. For Insta-Millionaires, this means a lower barrier to entry and the potential for higher returns on investment, as they leverage these cutting-edge tools to build their personal brands and monetize their social media presence.

Social media platforms have become the ultimate showcase for AI-generated supermodels, transforming the way they engage with followers. These virtual celebrities can participate in campaigns, interact with fans, and even create unique content that feels authentic and relatable. As they gain traction, they become trendsetters, influencing fashion and lifestyle choices on a massive scale. For aspiring Insta-Millionaires, aligning with these digital figures offers a chance to ride the wave of their popularity, driving traffic and engagement to their profiles while capitalizing on the growing trend of virtual influencers.

As we look toward the future, the evolution of modeling in the digital age promises to bring even more exciting developments. The integration of augmented reality and immersive experiences means that audiences will soon interact with virtual supermodels in ways we can only imagine today. This ongoing transformation opens up an array of possibilities for monetization, collaboration, and innovation. For those ready to embrace this new frontier, the potential to thrive as an Insta-Millionaire is limitless, fueled by the captivating allure of AI-generated supermodels that are reshaping the landscape of social media and beyond.

What Makes AI Supermodels Unique?

AI supermodels are revolutionizing the world of social media, bringing an unprecedented level of uniqueness and appeal that traditional models simply cannot match. One of the most compelling aspects of these digital dynamos is their ability to be entirely customizable. Brands can tailor every detail of an AI supermodel's appearance, personality, and style to resonate with their target audience. This flexibility allows for endless creativity, enabling companies to craft a character that aligns perfectly with their marketing goals, ensuring they stand out in a crowded digital marketplace.

Another factor that sets AI supermodels apart is their 24/7 availability and the sheer volume of content they can produce. Unlike human models, who have physical and time constraints, AI can generate an endless stream of stunning visuals, engaging videos, and interactive content at any hour. This capability means that brands can maintain a consistent online presence, engaging with their audience continuously and driving higher levels of interaction. The result is a dynamic and ever-evolving brand narrative that keeps followers coming back for more.

AI supermodels also bring a unique blend of style and trend adaptability to the table. They can effortlessly change their looks, outfits, and personas to keep up with the latest fashion trends and cultural shifts. This versatility not only keeps the content fresh and exciting but also positions brands as leaders in innovation and trendsetting. By harnessing the power of AI, brands can respond to market changes almost instantaneously, ensuring they are always ahead of the curve and appealing to their digital-savvy audience.

Moreover, AI supermodels offer a level of engagement that can be finely tuned to meet the desires of their followers. They can interact with audiences in real-time, responding to comments, participating in challenges, or even hosting virtual events. This interactivity fosters a sense of community and loyalty among fans, creating a deep emotional connection that translates to higher engagement rates and increased profitability. The ability to nurture relationships in such a personalized manner is a game changer for brands looking to capitalize on the influencer economy.

Finally, the ethical implications surrounding AI supermodels add another layer of uniqueness to their appeal. As the conversation about body positivity and diversity continues to grow, AI models can embody any aesthetic without the limitations or controversies often associated with human models. This opens the door for representations that celebrate all forms of beauty, potentially leading to a more inclusive digital landscape. Brands that leverage this aspect can position themselves as socially responsible and forward-thinking, attracting a broader audience while driving profitability in the process.

The Impact of Social Media on the Modeling Industry

The rise of social media has fundamentally transformed the modeling industry, offering unprecedented opportunities for aspiring models and established professionals alike. Platforms like Instagram, TikTok, and Snapchat have become the new catwalks, where followers can engage with models in real-time. This shift has allowed models to cultivate their personal brands, showcasing their unique styles and personalities to a global audience. The democratization of fashion means that anyone with a smartphone can step into the spotlight, creating a vibrant ecosystem where talent and creativity reign supreme. Now more than ever, social media is the gateway to fame and fortune in the modeling world.

In this digital age, traditional modeling agencies no longer hold monopoly power. Social media influencers and AI-generated supermodels are reshaping the landscape, challenging established norms. With millions of followers, these influencers can attract lucrative brand partnerships, often surpassing the earnings of their agency-represented counterparts. The allure of instant fame has led to an influx of content creators, each vying for attention while leveraging their social media presence to negotiate better deals and collaborations. This new dynamic empowers models to take charge of their careers, allowing them to monetize their digital personas in ways that were previously unimaginable.

Moreover, social media platforms have become essential marketing tools for brands seeking to connect with younger, tech-savvy consumers. Brands are increasingly turning to social media influencers to promote their products, recognizing the authenticity and relatability that comes with influencer marketing. This trend has accelerated the rise of niche models who cater to specific audiences, demonstrating that diversity and inclusion are not just buzzwords but essential elements of modern marketing strategies. As a result, models can carve out unique spaces for themselves, aligning with brands that resonate with their personal values and aesthetics.

AI-generated supermodels are also making waves in this new digital landscape. These virtual beings are not only visually stunning but also capable of engaging with fans around the clock. They can be programmed to embody various styles and personas, making them versatile assets for brands. The intersection of AI and social media has given rise to a new form of modeling that blurs the lines between reality and virtuality. As consumers become more accustomed to interacting with digital influencers, the potential for profit in this realm is staggering. Insta-millionaires who capitalize on this trend will find themselves at the forefront of a modeling revolution.

Ultimately, the impact of social media on the modeling industry is profound and ongoing. It fosters an environment where creativity flourishes, allowing for new voices to emerge and redefine beauty standards. As aspiring models and entrepreneurs embrace these digital platforms, they are not only reshaping their careers but also the entire modeling landscape. The fusion of social media, influencer culture, and AI-generated supermodels presents a thrilling frontier for those ready to seize the moment. With determination and innovation, anyone can become an Insta-millionaire, riding the wave of this exhilarating new era in modeling.

Chapter 2: Understanding AI Technology

The Basics of Artificial Intelligence

Artificial Intelligence (AI) is revolutionizing the way we interact with technology, and it has become an essential tool for anyone looking to succeed in the fast-paced world of social media. At its core, AI refers to the simulation of human intelligence processes by machines, particularly computer systems. These processes include learning, reasoning, and self-correction, enabling AI to analyze vast amounts of data at incredible speeds. For aspiring Insta-Millionaires, understanding these basics can unlock countless opportunities to leverage AI-generated supermodels for massive profits on social platforms.

One of the most exciting aspects of AI is its ability to create hyper-realistic images and videos that can mimic human models. With advanced algorithms, AI can generate stunning visuals that capture attention and engage audiences like never before. These AI-generated supermodels can be tailored to fit specific brand identities, target demographics, and social media trends, allowing businesses to craft personalized marketing strategies that resonate with potential customers. The result? An innovative way to promote products and services without the traditional costs associated with hiring human models.

Moreover, AI's capabilities extend beyond mere image generation. Machine learning, a subset of AI, enables systems to learn from data and improve their performance over time. This means that the more you use AI tools to analyze social media metrics, the better your strategies can become. By understanding audience preferences, engagement patterns, and trending topics, you can tailor your content to maximize reach and impact. For the Insta-Millionaire, this data-driven approach provides a significant competitive edge, transforming insights into actionable strategies that can drive exponential growth.

Another fascinating element of AI is its ability to automate processes, saving time and resources for creators and marketers. From content generation to customer interactions, AI tools can handle a range of tasks, allowing you to focus on what truly matters: building your brand and engaging with your audience. Chatbots, for example, can manage inquiries and provide instant responses, ensuring that potential customers feel valued and connected. This level of automation not only enhances efficiency but also fosters a seamless experience for your followers, ultimately leading to higher conversion rates.

In conclusion, grasping the basics of artificial intelligence is crucial for anyone looking to thrive in the world of AI-generated supermodels on social media. The combination of stunning visuals, data-driven insights, and automation offers a unique opportunity to create compelling content that captivates audiences. By embracing these technologies, you can position yourself at the forefront of this new frontier, transforming your passion for social media into a lucrative venture. The time to dive into the world of AI is now, and the possibilities are endless for those ready to take the plunge!

How AI Generates Photorealistic Models

Artificial Intelligence has revolutionized the way we create and visualize images, leading to the emergence of photorealistic models that captivate audiences on social media. By leveraging advanced algorithms and deep learning techniques, AI can generate lifelike images that often blur the lines between reality and the digital world. These models are not just visually stunning; they offer endless possibilities for brands and influencers looking to enhance their online presence and engage followers in unprecedented ways.

The process begins with extensive training on vast datasets of real human images. AI systems analyze facial structures, skin textures, and even subtle expressions to understand what makes a face appealing. This meticulous training allows the AI to learn the nuances of human features, enabling it to create models that are not only beautiful but also relatable. The result is a generation of digital personas that can express a wide range of emotions, making them perfect for marketing campaigns and social media interactions.

Once the AI has honed its skills, it can generate photorealistic models at lightning speed. This rapid production cycle means that businesses can quickly adapt to trends and create content that resonates with their audience. Imagine launching a new product with a stunning AI-generated supermodel who embodies the brand's ethos and appeals to the target demographic. The ability to produce high-quality visuals on demand is a game-changer, allowing brands to maintain a fresh and engaging online presence without the logistical headaches of traditional modeling.

Moreover, AI-generated models can be customized to fit specific themes or campaigns, making them incredibly versatile. Whether it's a fashion shoot, a lifestyle brand promotion, or an artistic project, these digital stars can be tailored to match any aesthetic or concept. This level of customization not only enhances creativity but also provides a unique opportunity for companies to tell their brand story in a visually compelling way. As businesses embrace this technology, the potential for innovative marketing strategies becomes virtually limitless.

In the world of social media, where first impressions are everything, AI-generated photorealistic models stand out as a bold new frontier. They offer a unique blend of creativity, efficiency, and engagement that traditional models simply cannot match. For aspiring Insta-Millionaires, harnessing the power of AI can lead to lucrative opportunities, transforming the way they approach branding and audience interaction. By embracing these cutting-edge technologies, anyone can step into the spotlight and capitalize on the captivating allure of AI-generated supermodels.

The Role of Machine Learning in Fashion

The integration of machine learning into the fashion industry has transformed the way brands operate, design, and connect with their consumers. As we step into an era dominated by digital interaction, machine learning algorithms are becoming essential tools for understanding consumer preferences and trends. This technology analyzes vast amounts of data to predict fashion trends, enabling brands to stay ahead of the curve. By leveraging these insights, fashion companies can create collections that resonate with their target audience, ensuring their designs are not only on point but also commercially viable.

One of the most exciting applications of machine learning in fashion is its ability to personalize shopping experiences. AI algorithms can track user behavior, preferences, and purchase histories to curate tailored recommendations. This level of personalization enhances customer satisfaction and loyalty, ultimately driving sales. Imagine an online store where every visitor is greeted with a selection of items specifically chosen for them, based on their previous interactions. This not only elevates the shopping experience but also boosts the likelihood of conversions, making it a win-win for both consumers and brands.

In addition to enhancing consumer experiences, machine learning plays a pivotal role in optimizing supply chains. By analyzing data related to inventory levels, production times, and shipping logistics, brands can streamline their processes, reducing costs and increasing efficiency. This is especially important in an industry that thrives on speed and responsiveness. The ability to predict demand accurately means that companies can produce the right amount of stock at the right time, minimizing waste and maximizing profitability. For aspiring Insta-millionaires, understanding and utilizing these efficiencies can significantly impact their bottom line.

Machine learning is also revolutionizing marketing strategies within the fashion sector. Social media platforms, where many Insta-millionaires find their success, are rich with data that can be harnessed through AI tools. These tools can analyze engagement metrics, audience demographics, and content performance to craft highly effective marketing campaigns. By understanding what resonates with their audience, brands can create targeted ads that drive engagement and conversions, ultimately building a more substantial following and, consequently, a more lucrative business model.

Lastly, the rise of AI-generated supermodels is a testament to the power of machine learning in redefining beauty standards and representation in fashion. These digital personas not only showcase clothing but also embody diversity and inclusivity in ways that traditional models may not. By utilizing AI to create and promote these supermodels, brands can connect with a broader audience and challenge conventional norms. For Insta-millionaires, embracing and promoting AI-generated supermodels can pave the way for innovative marketing strategies that highlight their brand's commitment to modernization and inclusivity, positioning them as leaders in the evolving landscape of fashion.

Chapter 3: The Insta-Millionaire Phenomenon

Defining the Insta-Millionaire Lifestyle

The Insta-Millionaire lifestyle is an exhilarating blend of glamour, innovation, and relentless ambition that has taken the digital world by storm. At its core, this lifestyle is defined by the seamless integration of cutting-edge technology with the allure of social media fame. Imagine waking up in a luxurious penthouse surrounded by stunning views, your morning coffee served by a virtual assistant, and the knowledge that your AI-generated supermodel is working tirelessly to engage millions of followers while you plan your next big venture. This is not just a dream; it is the exhilarating reality for those who embrace the Insta-Millionaire phenomenon.

Living the Insta-Millionaire lifestyle means harnessing the power of AI to create captivating content that resonates with audiences around the globe. AI-generated supermodels are revolutionizing the way brands connect with consumers, offering an endless stream of high-quality visuals and engaging narratives that traditional models simply cannot match. These digital personas live on social media platforms, captivating followers with their unique style and charisma. The Insta-Millionaire recognizes the immense potential in this technology, leveraging it to build an empire that thrives on creativity and innovation.

The financial rewards of the Insta-Millionaire lifestyle are as enticing as the lifestyle itself. With every post, collaboration, and sponsorship, opportunities for monetization expand exponentially.

Brands are eager to partner with those who can effectively use AI-generated content to drive engagement and sales. The ability to create eye-catching visuals without the constraints of traditional modeling means that the potential for profit is virtually limitless. This is a world where creativity meets commerce, and those who can navigate it successfully will reap the benefits of their ingenuity.

Community and connection are also vital elements of the Insta-Millionaire lifestyle. Building a loyal following requires more than just stunning visuals; it demands authenticity and engagement. Insta-Millionaires understand the importance of cultivating relationships with their audience, responding to comments, and creating a sense of belonging. By fostering this community, they not only enhance their brand but also create a network of support that can lead to new opportunities and collaborations. It's about creating a digital family that grows together, thriving in the exciting world of social media.

Ultimately, defining the Insta-Millionaire lifestyle is about embracing the future with open arms. It is an exhilarating journey that combines the thrill of financial success, the creativity of AI technology, and the joy of connecting with a global audience. As the landscape of social media continues to evolve, so too does the concept of success. For those willing to take the plunge, the Insta-Millionaire lifestyle offers a remarkable opportunity to redefine what it means to be successful in today's digital age. Embrace the adventure, unleash your creativity, and watch as your vision transforms into reality.

Case Studies of Successful Insta-Millionaires

In the dazzling world of social media, the rise of Insta-millionaires has captured the imagination of aspiring entrepreneurs everywhere. Among these trailblazers, several individuals have successfully harnessed the power of AI-generated supermodels, transforming their passion into lucrative businesses. These case studies not only highlight their innovative strategies but also serve as a source of inspiration for anyone looking to carve their own path in this exciting frontier.

Take the story of Sarah Lin, who first ventured into the realm of AI supermodels as a side project while juggling her full-time job. By creating a stunning AI-generated persona named Lila, she managed to capture the attention of thousands on Instagram. Sarah's keen insight into social media trends allowed her to cultivate Lila's image around luxury fashion and lifestyle. Collaborating with brands that aligned with Lila's aesthetic resulted in a flood of sponsorship deals, turning her side project into a profitable venture. Today, Sarah has transitioned to full-time entrepreneurship, showcasing the immense potential of AI supermodels in brand partnerships.

Another remarkable example is that of Mark Thompson, a tech-savvy marketer who stumbled upon the concept of AI-generated models during his quest for unique content creation. Mark designed a virtual influencer called Alex, whose adventurous spirit resonated with travel enthusiasts across various platforms. By leveraging AI's ability to produce stunning visual content, Mark crafted an engaging narrative around Alex's journeys. This captivating storytelling not only grew Alex's following exponentially but also attracted travel brands eager to collaborate. Mark's strategic approach exemplifies how blending creativity with technology can lead to extraordinary financial success.

Equally inspiring is the journey of Mia Patel, a graphic designer who recognized a gap in the beauty industry for diverse representations. She created an AI supermodel named Zuri, representing a blend of cultures and styles. Mia's commitment to inclusivity struck a chord with audiences, leading to viral content that resonated with many. Through partnerships with beauty brands that share her vision, Mia turned Zuri into a powerful voice for representation in an industry that often overlooks diversity. Her story underscores the importance of authenticity and purpose in building a brand around AI-generated personas.

These case studies illustrate not just the success of individual Insta-millionaires but also a burgeoning movement empowered by technology. The ability to create unique, engaging content through AI-generated supermodels is reshaping the landscape of social media marketing. For aspiring entrepreneurs, these stories are a testament to what is possible when creativity meets technology. By embracing the innovative tools available today, anyone can embark on their journey towards becoming the next Insta-millionaire, riding the wave of this thrilling new frontier.

The Business of Influence: How to Monetize Your Brand

The rise of AI-generated supermodels has transformed the landscape of social media, opening up unprecedented opportunities for monetization. As an Insta-Millionaire, you have the chance to harness the power of these digital personas to create a brand that resonates with millions. The business of influence is not just about having followers; it's about building a community that values your unique perspective and the products you promote. Understanding how to leverage AI-generated supermodels can give you a competitive edge that sets you apart in the crowded digital marketplace.

First and foremost, creating a compelling brand identity is essential. Your AI supermodel should embody the values and aesthetics that appeal to your target audience. This means curating a consistent visual style and voice that reflect your brand's ethos. Engage with your followers by sharing behind-the-scenes content, showcasing the creative process of your supermodel, and inviting them into your world. The more authentic and relatable your brand feels, the more likely your audience will be to invest in what you have to offer. Remember, your brand is not just a product; it's a lifestyle that followers want to be part of.

Monetization strategies for your AI supermodel can take many forms. Affiliate marketing is an excellent starting point, allowing you to earn commissions by promoting products that align with your brand. Choose brands that resonate with your audience and seamlessly integrate them into your content. Additionally, sponsored posts provide another lucrative avenue. Brands are eager to collaborate with influencers who can reach their desired demographics. By positioning your AI supermodel as a trusted voice in the industry, you can attract sponsorship deals that not only provide financial rewards but also enhance your credibility.

Beyond traditional monetization methods, consider creating exclusive content or experiences for your most dedicated followers. Platforms like Patreon or subscription-based services allow you to offer premium content, such as personalized styling advice or behind-the-scenes access to your creative process. This not only generates recurring revenue but also fosters a deeper connection with your audience. By providing value that goes beyond typical social media interactions, you can transform your followers into loyal, paying fans who are invested in your success.

Lastly, never underestimate the power of networking and collaboration. The influencer landscape thrives on partnerships, and by connecting with other creators, you can expand your reach exponentially. Participate in collaborative projects, cross-promote with fellow influencers, and explore joint ventures that can introduce your AI supermodel to new audiences. The more you engage with the community, the more opportunities will arise to monetize your brand. Remember, in this thrilling journey of cultivating your influence, the key to success lies in creativity, authenticity, and the relentless pursuit of connection. Embrace the possibilities and watch your brand soar to new heights!

Chapter 4: Creating Your AI Supermodel

Choosing the Right AI Tools and Platforms

Choosing the right AI tools and platforms is a crucial step for anyone looking to harness the power of AI-generated supermodels on social media. With an abundance of options available, it's essential to approach this decision with a clear understanding of your goals and the specific features that will help you achieve them. The right tools can elevate your brand, streamline your content creation process, and ultimately drive your success as an Insta-Millionaire.

Start by identifying the core functionalities you need. Are you looking for advanced image generation capabilities, realistic animation features, or seamless integration with social media platforms? Some AI tools specialize in hyper-realistic image creation, while others excel at producing engaging video content. By pinpointing your primary needs, you can narrow down your options and focus on platforms that align with your vision. Consider also the user-friendliness of these tools; you want an intuitive interface that allows you to hit the ground running without a steep learning curve.

Next, delve into the community and support surrounding each platform. A vibrant user community can provide invaluable insights, tips, and shared experiences that enhance your learning curve. Look for platforms that offer comprehensive tutorials, responsive customer support, and active forums where you can connect with other users. Engaging with a community can not only boost your confidence but also inspire creative ideas and collaborative opportunities.

Remember, the more resources you have at your disposal, the more successful you can be in leveraging AI-generated content.

Additionally, consider the scalability of the tools and platforms you choose. As your Insta-Millionaire journey progresses, your needs will evolve. Select tools that can grow with you, offering advanced features or higher processing power as you expand your social media presence. Whether you're starting with a single AI-generated model or planning to create a diverse roster of supermodels, ensure that your chosen platform can accommodate your future ambitions without requiring a complete overhaul.

Finally, don't forget to prioritize affordability and value. While some AI tools come with a hefty price tag, others offer competitive pricing with robust features. Evaluate the cost against the potential return on investment. As you navigate this exciting landscape, remember that the right AI tools and platforms will not only enhance your creative output but also empower you to connect with audiences in ways that were previously unimaginable. Choose wisely, and watch as your Insta-Millionaire dreams come to life!

Designing Your Supermodel's Aesthetic

Designing your supermodel's aesthetic is an exhilarating journey that merges creativity with cutting-edge technology. As you delve into this exciting process, you'll discover that the visual identity of your AI-generated supermodel is crucial in capturing the hearts of followers and attracting lucrative brand partnerships. The aesthetic encompasses everything from their clothing style and makeup to the environments they inhabit in their digital presence. This is your opportunity to unleash your imagination and craft a persona that resonates with audiences on social media, making your supermodel not just a face, but a brand that embodies aspirational living.

Start by defining the core elements of your supermodel's aesthetic. Consider the target audience you want to engage. Are they fashion-forward millennials, eco-conscious consumers, or luxury seekers?

Each demographic has unique preferences that can guide your design choices. Think about color palettes, textures, and themes that align with the lifestyle aspirations of your audience. For example, a vibrant and eclectic aesthetic might appeal to the adventurous spirit, while a minimalist and sophisticated look could attract a more refined clientele. This foundational step sets the stage for a cohesive image that will be recognizable across platforms.

Next, let's explore the importance of storytelling within your supermodel's aesthetic. Every image shared should convey a narrative that captivates viewers and encourages them to invest emotionally in your supermodel's journey. Use visual storytelling techniques to create scenarios that illustrate lifestyle aspirations, from glamorous red carpets to serene beach getaways. This not only enhances engagement but also opens the door for collaborations with brands that want to align with the lifestyle you portray. Remember, authenticity is key; your supermodel should embody a believable yet aspirational lifestyle that followers relate to and desire.

Incorporate the latest trends and technological advancements into your design process. The world of social media is ever-evolving, and staying ahead of trends can give your supermodel a competitive edge. Utilize AI tools to analyze popular aesthetics and emerging styles within your niche. This data-driven approach enables you to adapt your supermodel's image in real-time, ensuring that they remain relevant and appealing. Additionally, consider experimenting with augmented reality features, allowing followers to interact with your supermodel's aesthetic in innovative ways, further enhancing their connection to the brand.

Finally, consistency is the secret ingredient that binds your supermodel's aesthetic together. Establish a visual style guide that outlines key elements such as color schemes, fonts, and image composition. This guide will serve as a blueprint for all future content, ensuring that your supermodel's presence remains cohesive and instantly recognizable. Regularly assess and refine this aesthetic to keep it fresh and aligned with audience expectations. By maintaining a strong, consistent aesthetic, your AI-generated supermodel will not only attract followers but also establish a lasting brand that thrives in the competitive landscape of social media.

Developing a Unique Brand Identity

Developing a unique brand identity is the cornerstone of success in the world of AI-generated supermodels on social media. As an Insta-Millionaire, you must harness the power of AI to create images and personas that resonate with your target audience. This involves more than just generating stunning visuals; it's about crafting a narrative that reflects your values and appeals to the emotions of your followers. Your brand identity should encapsulate what makes you distinct, allowing your audience to connect with you on a personal level, which is essential for building loyalty and trust.

To start, identify the key attributes that you want your brand to embody. These could range from elegance and sophistication to boldness and creativity. Consider how these attributes align with the AI-generated supermodels you plan to feature. Use these characteristics as a foundation for your messaging, visuals, and overall aesthetic. Consistency is key; when your audience knows what to expect from your brand, they are more likely to engage and share your content. This familiarity will help you cultivate a community around your brand, turning casual followers into dedicated fans.

Next, leverage storytelling to enrich your brand identity. In the realm of social media, storytelling can transform a simple image into an engaging narrative that captivates your audience. Share the journey behind the AI supermodels, their creation, and the inspiration that drives your brand. Use captions and posts to convey stories that resonate with your followers' aspirations, dreams, and values. This emotional connection not only makes your brand more relatable but also encourages your audience to invest in your vision, leading to increased engagement and profitability.

Visual elements play a crucial role in establishing a memorable brand identity. Ensure that your color palette, typography, and design elements reflect the unique essence of your brand. Collaborate with talented graphic designers who understand the aesthetics of social media and can help elevate your visual impact. High-quality imagery of your AI supermodels can set you apart in a crowded digital landscape. By maintaining a cohesive visual style across all platforms, you solidify your brand identity and make it easily recognizable, enhancing your chances of attracting followers and potential customers.

Finally, engage with your audience authentically. Building a unique brand identity is not a one-way street; it requires active participation and interaction. Respond to comments, ask for feedback, and encourage your followers to share their thoughts and experiences related to your content. This two-way communication fosters a sense of belonging and loyalty among your followers. As you develop your brand identity, remember that it should evolve over time, reflecting changes in trends, audience preferences, and your own growth as an Insta-Millionaire. Embrace this journey, and let your unique brand identity shine as you navigate the exciting world of AI-generated supermodels on social media.

Chapter 5: Building an Engaging Social Media Presence

Selecting the Right Platforms for Your Audience

Selecting the right platforms for your audience is crucial in the journey towards becoming an Insta-Millionaire. With countless social media platforms available, it can be overwhelming to determine where to focus your efforts. The key is to identify where your target audience spends their time and engages most actively. For aspiring entrepreneurs in the realm of AI-generated supermodels, platforms like Instagram, TikTok, and even YouTube are essential. Each platform offers unique features and demographics that can elevate your brand and connect with potential clients and followers.

Instagram remains the powerhouse for visual content, making it an ideal platform for showcasing AI-generated supermodels. With its emphasis on stunning imagery and aesthetics, you can create a compelling portfolio that captures attention and drives engagement. Utilize Instagram Stories and Reels to showcase behind-the-scenes content and the creative process behind your supermodels. This not only builds interest but also humanizes your brand, allowing followers to connect on a deeper level. Engaging with your audience through comments and direct messages enhances your community, turning casual viewers into loyal fans.

TikTok is another vibrant platform that cannot be overlooked. Its short-form video format allows for creative storytelling and rapid content consumption, making it perfect for showcasing the dynamic and innovative aspects of AI-generated supermodels. Trends on TikTok can explode overnight, offering a unique opportunity to reach a wide audience. By participating in challenges, using popular sounds, and creating captivating content, you can tap into viral marketing strategies that boost your visibility. Remember, authenticity is key on this platform, so let your personality shine through in every video.

YouTube serves as a fantastic avenue for deeper engagement and storytelling. As a longer-form content platform, it allows you to explore the intricacies of your AI supermodels and share valuable insights about the technology behind them. Tutorials, behind-the-scenes videos, and interviews with industry experts can position you as a thought leader in the niche. By building a subscriber base on YouTube, you create a loyal audience that is eager to learn more about your offerings. This platform also opens doors for monetization through ads and partnerships, adding another revenue stream to your Insta-Millionaire journey.

Ultimately, understanding your audience's behavior on these platforms is vital for maximizing your impact. Regularly analyze metrics and adjust your strategy based on what resonates most with your followers. Experiment with different types of content and engagement tactics to see what drives the best results. By selecting the right platforms and tailoring your approach to each, you set yourself up for success in the competitive landscape of AI-generated supermodels. Embrace the excitement of exploring these platforms, and watch as your Insta-Millionaire dreams turn into reality!

Crafting Captivating Content

Crafting captivating content is the cornerstone of building a successful presence on social media, especially when leveraging AI-generated supermodels. In a landscape where attention spans are short and competition is fierce, your content needs to dazzle and engage. The beauty of AI-generated supermodels lies not only in their stunning visuals but also in the endless creative possibilities they present. By harnessing these capabilities, you can create content that resonates deeply with your audience and elevates your brand to new heights.

Start by understanding your audience's desires and aspirations. What makes them tick? What challenges do they face, and how can your content provide solutions? AI-generated supermodels can embody various personas, styles, and moods, allowing you to tailor your content to speak directly to your target demographic. Whether your audience craves high fashion, relatable lifestyle moments, or aspirational travel, these digital personas can bring your vision to life, creating a connection that feels personal and authentic.

Next, focus on storytelling. Every piece of content should tell a story that captivates viewers from the first glance. Use your AI supermodels to craft narratives that evoke emotion, whether it's joy, nostalgia, or inspiration. By integrating storytelling elements into your posts—be it through captions, videos, or an entire series—you create a cohesive narrative that encourages your audience to engage, share, and return for more. This approach transforms your content from mere visuals into an immersive experience that keeps followers coming back.

Don't underestimate the power of collaboration. The digital world is all about synergy, and pairing your AI-generated supermodels with influencers or brands that align with your vision can amplify your message. Collaborations can introduce your content to new audiences and create buzz that propels you forward. Think creatively about how these partnerships can enhance your storytelling, whether through joint campaigns, challenges, or interactive content that invites audience participation.

Finally, keep experimenting and analyzing your results. The beauty of crafting content in the digital age is the wealth of data at your fingertips. Use analytics to understand what resonates with your audience, and don't be afraid to pivot your strategy based on those insights. Embrace trends, but stay true to your brand's unique voice. By continually refining your approach and staying agile, you'll ensure that your content remains captivating, fresh, and aligned with the ever-evolving preferences of your audience. In this dynamic landscape, the possibilities for success are limitless, and your journey to Insta-Millionaire status is just beginning!

Leveraging Trends and Viral Marketing

In the fast-paced world of social media, staying ahead of trends is not just advantageous; it's essential for success. Leveraging trends and viral marketing can catapult your AI-generated supermodel into the spotlight, attracting followers and generating revenue like never before. The beauty of social media is its dynamic nature, where one moment can change everything. By harnessing the power of trending topics, challenges, and hashtags, you can create content that resonates with audiences and encourages engagement. This is your opportunity to ride the wave of popularity and turn fleeting moments into lasting success.

To effectively tap into viral marketing, understanding your audience is crucial. What excites them? What are they sharing? By analyzing social media conversations and current events, you can identify key trends that align with your AI supermodel's brand. This strategy not only increases visibility but also fosters a sense of connection with your followers. When your content reflects their interests and desires, they are more likely to engage, share, and even become loyal customers. Remember, authenticity is key; your AI supermodel should embody the traits and trends that resonate most with your target demographic.

Content creation is where the magic happens. Utilize eye-catching visuals, catchy captions, and relatable narratives that align with trending themes. Whether it's participating in viral challenges or creating memes that play off popular culture, the goal is to generate buzz and encourage sharing. Collaborating with influencers or other trending personalities can also amplify your reach, introducing your AI supermodel to new audiences. The more engaging and entertaining your content, the higher the chances of it going viral. Think outside the box and don't be afraid to experiment with different formats such as videos, stories, or live streams.

Timing is everything in the realm of viral marketing. Being quick to react to emerging trends can set you apart from the competition. Use social media analytics tools to monitor trending topics in real time, allowing you to jump on opportunities as they arise. A timely post can turn your AI supermodel into a household name overnight. Additionally, consider creating a content calendar that incorporates both planned posts and spontaneous content that aligns with current trends. This dual approach ensures that you remain relevant while being flexible enough to capitalize on unexpected opportunities.

Lastly, don't underestimate the power of community. Engaging with your audience through comments, direct messages, and interactive polls can foster a loyal following that actively participates in your brand's journey. Encourage your followers to share their own content related to your AI supermodel, creating a sense of ownership and belonging. By building a vibrant community around your brand, you turn casual viewers into enthusiastic advocates who will spread the word about your AI supermodel, driving even more traffic and potential profits. Embrace the trends, unleash your creativity, and watch as your AI supermodel thrives in the ever-evolving landscape of social media.

Chapter 6: Strategies for Monetization

Affiliate Marketing with AI Supermodels

Affiliate marketing has evolved dramatically with the emergence of AI supermodels, creating a new frontier for aspiring Insta-millionaires. Imagine leveraging the captivating allure of AI-generated personas to promote products and services that resonate with your audience. These digital supermodels, designed to be visually stunning and engaging, are not just a fad; they represent a groundbreaking opportunity to tap into lucrative affiliate marketing strategies. By aligning with brands that complement your AI supermodel's persona, you can create a seamless promotional experience that drives conversions and boosts your income.

The key to successful affiliate marketing with AI supermodels lies in authenticity and relatability. While these digital beings are crafted from advanced algorithms and stunning graphics, they can still connect with audiences on a personal level. By curating content that feels genuine and resonates with your followers, you can effectively promote products that reflect your supermodel's character. This approach not only enhances engagement but also fosters trust, making your audience more likely to act on your recommendations. Remember, the more relatable your AI supermodel is, the more successful your affiliate marketing efforts will be.

Utilizing social media platforms is essential in maximizing the reach of your AI supermodel's affiliate marketing campaigns. Platforms like Instagram, TikTok, and even YouTube are perfect for showcasing your supermodel in action, promoting products through dynamic visuals and engaging stories. Create eye-catching posts, reels, and videos that highlight the products in a natural setting, allowing your audience to envision how these items fit into their lives. The power of visual storytelling can significantly amplify your affiliate links, leading to increased traffic and conversions.

Moreover, collaboration with brands is a vital aspect of affiliate marketing success. Seek out partnerships with companies that align with your AI supermodel's niche and aesthetic. Whether it's fashion, beauty, tech, or fitness, choose brands that resonate with your audience's interests. This strategic alignment will enhance the credibility of your promotions and ensure that your followers see the value in your recommendations. The more authentic the partnership, the more effective your affiliate marketing efforts will be.

Finally, tracking your performance and adapting your strategies is crucial in this fast-paced environment. Utilize analytics tools to monitor engagement, click-through rates, and conversion metrics. Understanding what works and what doesn't will help you refine your approach, enabling you to maximize your earnings over time. Stay ahead of trends and continuously innovate your content to keep your audience captivated. With the right strategies in place, affiliate marketing with AI supermodels can transform your social media presence into a powerful income-generating machine, paving your way to Insta-millionaire success.

Sponsored Content and Brand Partnerships

Sponsored content and brand partnerships represent a thrilling opportunity for Insta-Millionaires leveraging AI-generated supermodels on social media. As you dive into this new frontier, consider how these digital avatars can seamlessly integrate into marketing strategies that resonate with audiences. Gone are the days when traditional advertising felt intrusive; today's consumers crave authentic experiences, and AI supermodels can deliver just that. By collaborating with brands, you can create engaging content that feels organic and relatable, driving both visibility and revenue.

The beauty of AI-generated supermodels lies in their versatility. They can be tailored to embody various styles, personalities, and aesthetics that align perfectly with specific brand identities. Whether it's a luxury fashion label or an eco-friendly skincare line, these digital models can represent them in ways that feel fresh and innovative. The key is to ensure that the partnerships feel genuine and that the supermodels authentically reflect the brand's values. This alignment not only enhances credibility but also fosters a deeper connection with the target audience, leading to increased engagement and sales.

As an Insta-Millionaire, you have the unique advantage of being at the forefront of this trend. By strategically selecting brand partnerships that resonate with your audience, you can craft compelling narratives that captivate followers. Imagine a day in the life of your AI supermodel, showcasing products in a way that feels effortless and inspiring. This storytelling approach can transform sponsored content from mere advertisements into captivating visual experiences that encourage interaction and sharing, amplifying your reach and impact.

Moreover, the analytics provided by social media platforms allow you to track the performance of your sponsored content in real-time. You can see what resonates with your audience, refine your strategies, and optimize future brand collaborations. This data-driven approach not only maximizes your earnings but also helps you build long-lasting relationships with brands that want to harness the power of AI-generated supermodels. The insights gained can also inform how you create content that aligns with trending topics, ensuring you remain relevant in a fast-paced digital landscape.

In conclusion, embracing sponsored content and brand partnerships with AI supermodels opens up a world of possibilities for Insta-Millionaires. This innovative approach not only enhances your income streams but also allows you to shape the future of influencer marketing. By focusing on authenticity, creativity, and analytics, you can create a winning formula that captivates audiences, drives engagement, and ultimately propels your success in the ever-evolving world of social media. Your journey as an Insta-Millionaire has just begun, and the potential is limitless!

Creating Merchandise and Digital Products

Creating merchandise and digital products is an exhilarating way to capitalize on the unique allure of AI-generated supermodels. As an Insta-Millionaire, tapping into this potential can enhance your brand while generating a significant revenue stream. Imagine building a line of products that resonate with your audience, all inspired by the captivating imagery and personalities of AI supermodels. The key is to align your merchandise with the interests and desires of your followers, ensuring that each product feels like a natural extension of your digital persona.

Start by brainstorming merchandise ideas that reflect the essence of your AI supermodels. Apparel, accessories, and home decor items are just the tip of the iceberg. Consider creating limited-edition collections that showcase stunning visuals or quotes from your AI models. These exclusive items can create a sense of urgency among your audience, driving sales and fostering a loyal following. Collaborating with graphic designers or utilizing print-on-demand services can streamline the process, allowing you to focus on promoting your products while experts handle the logistics.

Digital products are another exciting avenue for revenue generation. Think e-books, courses, or even exclusive behind-the-scenes content featuring your AI supermodels. By sharing insights into the creative process or teaching your audience how to create their own digital content, you establish yourself as an authority in the field. This not only boosts your credibility but also deepens the connection with your audience, making them more likely to support your merchandise offerings.

Don't underestimate the power of social media in promoting your merchandise and digital products. Utilize the very platforms that propelled your AI supermodels to fame. Create engaging content that showcases your products in action, leverage storytelling to highlight their unique features, and don't forget to encourage user-generated content. When your audience shares their experiences with your merchandise, it amplifies your reach and builds a community around your brand.

Finally, make sure to regularly evaluate and adapt your offerings based on feedback and trends. The digital landscape is ever-evolving, and staying ahead of the curve is essential for sustained success. Engage with your audience to understand their preferences and interests, and don't hesitate to experiment with new product lines or digital offerings. By continuously innovating and listening to your community, you'll not only maintain their loyalty but also position yourself as a leading figure in the world of AI-generated supermodels. Embrace this thrilling journey, and watch your Insta-Millionaire dreams come to life!

Chapter 7: Legal Considerations

Copyright and Ownership of AI Creations

In the exhilarating world of AI-generated supermodels, understanding copyright and ownership is crucial for anyone looking to capitalize on this revolutionary technology. As you dive into the realm of AI creations, it's vital to grasp how intellectual property laws apply to these digital wonders. The unique blend of creativity and technology in AI-generated content raises questions about who truly owns the work. Is it the programmer, the user, or perhaps a collaboration between both? These considerations can make or break your journey toward becoming an Insta-Millionaire.

When you harness AI to produce stunning virtual models, you're tapping into a creative force that generates images, animations, and even videos that can captivate audiences and drive engagement. However, the complexity of copyright law means you need to be savvy about the rights associated with these creations. Generally, if you develop the AI and generate the artwork, you may claim ownership. But if you're simply using an AI tool created by someone else, the rules can get murky. Always check the terms of service of the AI platform you're using; many platforms retain some ownership rights or impose restrictions on commercial use.

It's also essential to recognize that the landscape of copyright is evolving, especially in light of AI advancements. As more artists and businesses leverage AI technology, legal frameworks are catching up. Courts are beginning to address questions about originality and authorship in the context of AI-generated works. This means that as an aspiring Insta-Millionaire, you should stay informed about the latest developments in copyright law. Staying ahead of these changes could give you a competitive edge and help you navigate potential legal pitfalls.

Moreover, consider the ethical implications of using AI-generated content. While the technology is groundbreaking, it can raise questions about authenticity and representation. Addressing these issues transparently can enhance your brand's credibility and appeal. When you create content featuring AI supermodels, think about how you position them in your marketing strategy. Representing diversity and inclusivity is not just ethically sound; it's also a savvy business move that resonates with today's audiences, making your brand more relatable and marketable.

Ultimately, the journey to Insta-Millionaire success in the age of AI supermodels hinges on understanding copyright and ownership dynamics. By educating yourself about your rights and responsibilities, you can harness the power of AI while safeguarding your creative endeavors. Embrace the potential of AI-generated content, but do so with a keen awareness of the legal landscape. This proactive approach will not only protect your assets but also empower you to innovate, allowing your brand to thrive in an exciting, rapidly evolving market.

Navigating Influencer Regulations

In the fast-paced world of social media, navigating influencer regulations is crucial for anyone looking to profit from AI-generated supermodels. As the landscape evolves, so do the rules governing how influencers and brands can operate. Understanding these regulations is not just about compliance; it's about leveraging them to enhance your brand's credibility and build trust with your audience. These guidelines can serve as a roadmap to ensure you're on the right track, allowing you to focus on what really matters: creating captivating content and driving engagement.

First and foremost, transparency is key. Regulations often mandate that influencers disclose their partnerships with brands or any sponsored content. This means that whether you're collaborating with a brand or promoting a product through an AI supermodel, you must clearly communicate this relationship to your followers. This transparency not only keeps you in compliance with the Federal Trade Commission (FTC) guidelines but also fosters a sense of authenticity. When your audience knows that you're upfront about your partnerships, they're more likely to trust your recommendations and engage with the content you create.

Next, it's essential to stay informed about the constantly changing regulations in the influencer marketing space. As new technologies emerge, so do new laws and guidelines. Subscribe to industry newsletters, attend webinars, and participate in online forums where influencer marketing is discussed. By staying ahead of the curve, you can adapt your strategies accordingly and avoid potential pitfalls. This proactive approach can also position you as a thought leader in the space, attracting more opportunities for collaboration and partnership.

Another important aspect of navigating influencer regulations involves understanding intellectual property rights. Using AI-generated supermodels can blur the lines when it comes to ownership and usage rights. Ensure that you have clear agreements in place regarding the use of images, videos, and other content. This not only protects you legally but also ensures that you respect the work of creators and brands you collaborate with. By establishing a solid foundation of respect and legality, you can build long-lasting relationships that are beneficial for everyone involved.

Lastly, engaging with your audience about these regulations can be a powerful tool. Share insights and information about your compliance practices, and encourage discussions around transparency in influencer marketing. This not only positions you as a responsible influencer but also educates your audience on the importance of ethical practices. By fostering a community that values authenticity and transparency, you're not just following regulations; you're paving the way for a more trustworthy and engaging social media environment. Embrace these regulations as part of your journey, and watch how they can enhance your brand's reputation while maximizing your success in the world of AI supermodels.

Protecting Your Brand from Imitation

In the exhilarating world of AI-generated supermodels, where creativity meets technology, protecting your brand from imitation is paramount. As you ride the wave of success on social media, the allure of your unique identity can attract others eager to replicate your formula. You've invested time, energy, and resources into building a brand that resonates with your audience, and the last thing you want is for someone to hijack that hard work. The first step in safeguarding your brand is understanding the landscape of intellectual property rights. Familiarize yourself with trademarks, copyrights, and other legal protections that can shield your innovative creations from being copied.

One of the most effective ways to fortify your brand is by establishing a strong online presence that showcases your originality. Engage with your audience through compelling content that highlights what makes your AI-generated supermodels unique. Share behind-the-scenes insights, success stories, and the creative process that differentiates your brand. The more authentic and transparent you are, the more your followers will connect with you, making it harder for imitators to eclipse your influence. Remember, in the age of social media, your personality and storytelling are just as crucial as the visuals you present.

Additionally, consider leveraging technology to monitor potential infringements. There are numerous tools available that can help you track the usage of your images and content across various platforms. Setting up alerts for your brand name, logos, and key phrases can help you catch unauthorized use before it spirals out of control. When you identify instances of imitation, take swift action to address them. Whether it's sending a friendly cease-and-desist letter or reporting the issue directly to the platform, being proactive shows that you take your brand seriously and won't tolerate unauthorized copying.

Collaboration is another powerful strategy to fortify your brand against imitation. Partnering with other creators, influencers, and brands can enhance your visibility and credibility, making it harder for imitators to gain traction. By fostering a strong network, you not only expand your reach but also create a supportive community that values originality. These alliances can lead to innovative projects that showcase your unique offerings, further solidifying your position in the market and reinforcing the idea that your brand is the original and the best.

Finally, continually innovate and evolve your brand. The digital landscape is ever-changing, and staying ahead of trends will keep your audience engaged and attract new followers. Experiment with new formats, styles, and collaborations that reflect the cutting-edge nature of AI-generated supermodels. By pushing the boundaries of creativity and staying relevant, you make it increasingly difficult for imitators to keep up. Remember, the key to protecting your brand from imitation lies not just in defending what you've built but in constantly creating and inspiring, ensuring that your brand remains at the forefront of the Insta-millionaire revolution.

Chapter 8: The Future of AI Supermodels

Trends Shaping the Future of Fashion and AI

The intersection of fashion and artificial intelligence is transforming the industry in exhilarating ways, creating a vibrant landscape ripe for innovation and profit. AI is not just a tool but a catalyst for change, reshaping how brands design, market, and engage with consumers. Fashion trends are now emerging faster than ever, driven by algorithms that analyze consumer behavior, predict preferences, and create personalized shopping experiences. With AI-generated supermodels at the forefront, the future of fashion is not just about garments; it's about crafting unique digital identities that resonate with audiences around the globe.

Social media platforms are becoming the playground for AI-driven fashion innovation. Brands are harnessing the power of AI to create hyper-targeted marketing campaigns that speak directly to individual consumers. This personalized approach not only increases engagement but also drives sales, as shoppers feel a deeper connection to the products being showcased. Insta-millionaires can capitalize on this trend by leveraging AI-generated supermodels to create captivating visuals and narratives that resonate with specific demographics. The ability to quickly adapt to trends and consumer feedback allows for a dynamic and profitable business model.

Moreover, the rise of virtual fashion shows and digital clothing is revolutionizing the way fashion is presented and consumed. AI technology enables designers to create stunning virtual collections that can be showcased online, eliminating the need for costly physical runway shows. This shift not only reduces overhead costs but opens up opportunities for accessibility as consumers from all over the world can experience new collections in real-time. Insta-millionaires can take advantage of this trend by curating exclusive virtual fashion events featuring AI-generated supermodels, thus creating buzz and driving sales in a way that traditional fashion shows could never achieve.

Sustainability is another pivotal trend shaping the future of fashion, and AI is playing a crucial role in this movement. By using data analytics and machine learning, brands can optimize their supply chains, reduce waste, and create more sustainable products. Consumers are increasingly drawn to brands that prioritize eco-friendly practices, and AI-generated supermodels can amplify these messages through powerful storytelling on social media. Insta-millionaires can become ambassadors for sustainability by collaborating with brands that leverage AI for ethical fashion, attracting a conscious consumer base and enhancing their brand image.

Finally, as fashion continues to embrace AI technology, the potential for collaboration between digital and physical worlds is limitless. From augmented reality fitting rooms to AI-driven design tools, the fashion landscape is evolving into a hybrid model that merges the best of both realms. Insta-millionaires can thrive in this environment by staying ahead of the curve, investing in AI technologies, and exploring innovative ways to engage their audiences. The future of fashion is not just bright; it's dazzling with possibilities, and those who embrace the trends shaping this new frontier will undoubtedly reap the rewards.

Sustainability and Ethical Considerations

Sustainability and ethical considerations are becoming increasingly vital in the world of AI-generated supermodels. As the Insta-Millionaire community continues to grow and thrive, the conversation around environmental responsibility and ethical practices must take center stage. These digital fashion icons may not have a physical presence, but their impact on the industry and society can be profound. Embracing sustainability not only enhances brand reputation but can also attract a more conscious audience eager to support responsible practices.

The allure of AI supermodels lies in their endless potential for creativity and engagement. However, as Insta-Millionaires, it's essential to recognize the ethical implications of using AI in fashion and advertising. The technology behind these virtual influencers raises questions about authenticity, representation, and the mental health of followers. By prioritizing transparency in how AI models are created and represented, you can build trust with your audience. This trust is invaluable, as consumers today are more discerning and increasingly demand accountability from brands.

Moreover, implementing sustainable practices in the digital modeling space can set you apart in a competitive market. Consider collaborating with eco-friendly brands or promoting sustainable fashion choices through your AI supermodels. By aligning your strategies with environmental consciousness, you not only cater to a growing demographic of eco-aware consumers but also contribute to a larger movement towards sustainability in the fashion industry.

This alignment can enhance your brand's appeal and lead to long-term success, proving that profitability and responsibility can coexist harmoniously.

Another key aspect of sustainability in the realm of AI supermodels is the potential to reduce waste. Traditional fashion shoots often involve excessive materials, transportation, and resource consumption. AI-generated models can disrupt this cycle by minimizing the need for physical products and locations. By embracing this innovative approach, you can advocate for a new era of fashion that prioritizes efficiency and eco-friendliness. This not only positions you as a leader in the industry but also aligns your brand with the values of a forward-thinking audience.

Finally, engaging with your audience on sustainability and ethical considerations can foster a more profound connection. Share stories about your commitment to responsible practices, showcase your partnerships with ethical brands, and invite your followers to participate in discussions about the future of fashion. By actively involving your community in these conversations, you create a loyal following that resonates with your mission and values. In doing so, you not only elevate your brand but also contribute to a brighter, more sustainable future for the fashion industry and beyond.

How AI Supermodels Will Transform the Industry

The rise of AI supermodels is set to revolutionize the fashion and social media industries like never before. Imagine a world where stunning, photogenic models are generated by algorithms, boasting flawless features and the ability to adapt to any brand's vision. This transformation offers an unprecedented opportunity for businesses and influencers alike. As these digital personas gain popularity, they will redefine traditional notions of beauty and representation, making it possible for anyone to leverage their appeal without the constraints of the physical world.

AI supermodels present a groundbreaking avenue for creativity and innovation in marketing strategies. Brands can now collaborate with these virtual entities to create tailored campaigns that resonate with their target audiences. With the ability to analyze vast amounts of data, AI can identify trends and preferences, allowing for more effective promotional content. This level of customization not only enhances engagement but also drives sales. Companies that embrace AI supermodels will find themselves at the forefront of a new era, where marketing campaigns are sharper, more dynamic, and highly appealing to consumers.

The financial implications of AI supermodels are staggering. By eliminating the need for physical models and associated costs, brands can significantly reduce their marketing expenses. Hiring, traveling, and managing human models can be resource-intensive, but with AI, these costs vanish. This newfound efficiency allows companies to reallocate funds towards more innovative projects or to improve their bottom lines. For aspiring Insta-millionaires, this means an easier pathway to success, as they can create and promote their own virtual models, turning them into marketable assets without the hefty price tag.

Social media is the perfect playground for AI supermodels to thrive. Their digital nature allows for seamless integration into various platforms, where they can engage with followers and create a buzz around products. With the right algorithms and creativity, these models can generate viral content that captivates audiences. Influencers and marketers can harness this potential by creating unique narratives around their AI supermodels, driving engagement and leading to increased brand loyalty. The interactive and visually stunning nature of AI supermodels will undoubtedly attract attention and propel them into the limelight of social media.

As we look to the future, the potential for AI supermodels is limitless. They are not just a passing trend; they represent a fundamental shift in how we perceive beauty and marketing. The ability to create diverse, inclusive, and relatable characters through AI technology will cater to a broader audience while empowering brands to tell compelling stories. For those ready to seize the moment, the rise of AI supermodels offers an exciting opportunity to redefine success in the digital age. By embracing this innovative frontier, Insta-millionaires can ride the wave of transformation and unlock new doors to financial prosperity.

Chapter 9: Success Stories and Interviews

Interviews with Leading Innovators

Interviews with leading innovators in the realm of AI-generated supermodels reveal a world brimming with creativity, ambition, and groundbreaking technology. These trailblazers are at the forefront of redefining beauty and influence in the digital landscape, and their insights are invaluable for anyone aiming to capitalize on this thrilling trend. As we dive into their experiences, we discover the exhilarating potential of AI to transform not just the fashion industry but also the very fabric of social media engagement.

One of the standout figures in this space is a visionary entrepreneur who has successfully integrated AI algorithms into the modeling process. During our conversation, they shared how these algorithms can analyze current trends, consumer preferences, and even cultural shifts, enabling the creation of supermodels that resonate with diverse audiences. This innovative approach not only streamlines the modeling process but also allows for rapid content generation, ensuring that brands remain relevant and captivating. For aspiring Insta-millionaires, the key takeaway is clear: leveraging AI technology can propel your brand to new heights.

Another inspiring innovator is a digital artist who has pioneered the art of crafting lifelike AI-generated models. Their passion for blending artistry with technology has led to the creation of stunning visuals that captivate followers and drive engagement. They emphasized the importance of storytelling in their work, noting that every supermodel they create has a unique narrative that enhances its appeal. For those looking to profit from this phenomenon, the message is loud and clear: don't just generate images; create characters that your audience can connect with on a personal level.

The discussions also highlighted the role of social media platforms in amplifying the reach of AI-generated supermodels. A social media strategist shared how brands that effectively utilize these digital personas have seen exponential growth in their follower counts and engagement rates. They advised aspiring Insta-millionaires to be strategic in their content distribution, utilizing analytics to understand what resonates with their audience. The more you understand your audience, the better you can tailor your approach, ensuring that your AI supermodels become not just figures of beauty but also icons of influence.

Lastly, the innovators unanimously pointed to the future of this industry as a canvas of endless possibilities. With advancements in AI technology continuing to accelerate, the potential for creating hyper-realistic models that can engage and inspire is greater than ever. As they shared their visions for the future, it became evident that the journey of integrating AI into the world of modeling is just beginning. For those ready to embark on this adventure, the insights from these leading innovators serve as both inspiration and a roadmap to success in the exhilarating world of AI-generated supermodels on social media.

Lessons Learned from Top AI Supermodel Creators

The world of AI-generated supermodels is not just a revolution in technology; it's a masterclass in innovation, creativity, and entrepreneurial spirit. Top creators in this space have shared invaluable lessons that can elevate aspiring Insta-Millionaires to new heights. One of the most significant takeaways is the importance of embracing technology with an open mind. By understanding the nuances of AI, creators can leverage tools that enhance their creativity rather than stifle it. This mindset allows for the exploration of limitless possibilities, transforming visions into digital realities that captivate audiences.

Another critical lesson is the power of collaboration. Successful AI supermodel creators often work with diverse teams, combining expertise in technology, fashion, marketing, and social media. This collaborative approach enables them to produce compelling content that resonates with followers and drives engagement. For budding entrepreneurs, the message is clear: don't hesitate to seek partnerships that can complement your skills and broaden your reach. By collaborating with others, you can tap into new perspectives and resources that can amplify your brand's presence in the crowded social media landscape.

Understanding your audience is paramount in this digital age. Top creators take the time to study trends, preferences, and behaviors of their followers. This insight allows them to tailor their content to meet the desires of their audience, creating a loyal fan base that eagerly anticipates each new post. For aspiring Insta-Millionaires, this means investing time in analytics and feedback mechanisms. By continuously refining your approach based on audience engagement, you can create a more impactful presence that not only attracts followers but also converts them into customers.

Consistency in branding and messaging is another vital lesson from leading creators. They establish a distinct identity for their AI supermodels, from visual aesthetics to tone of voice, ensuring that every piece of content aligns with their brand values. This uniformity fosters recognition and trust among followers, which is crucial for building a successful online presence. Newcomers to the Insta-Millionaire scene should focus on crafting a cohesive brand strategy that reflects their vision and resonates with their target audience, ultimately leading to increased profitability.

Lastly, adaptability is key in the fast-paced world of social media and AI. The most successful creators remain agile, pivoting their strategies as trends evolve and new technologies emerge. They are quick to experiment with different platforms, content formats, and marketing techniques, ensuring they stay ahead of the curve. As an aspiring Insta-Millionaire, cultivating a willingness to learn and adapt will empower you to navigate challenges and seize opportunities in this dynamic landscape. Embrace these lessons, and you'll be well on your way to becoming a trailblazer in the realm of AI-generated supermodels on social media.

Inspiring Stories of Transformation

In the dazzling world of social media, where likes and shares can skyrocket an individual into stardom overnight, the rise of AI-generated supermodels is nothing short of revolutionary. These digital darlings are not just a trend; they represent a seismic shift in how we perceive beauty, branding, and entrepreneurship. There are countless stories of individuals who have harnessed the power of AI-generated models to elevate their brands and transform their lives. These inspiring tales reveal the limitless possibilities that await those who dare to innovate and adapt in the ever-evolving landscape of digital marketing.

Consider the journey of a small-town fashion designer who was struggling to gain traction in a saturated market. With a passion for creativity but limited resources, they turned to AI-generated supermodels to showcase their unique designs. By creating stunning virtual campaigns featuring these models, they captured the attention of a global audience. The result? A meteoric rise in brand recognition and an influx of orders that transformed their humble venture into a thriving business. Their story exemplifies how embracing new technology can lead to extraordinary outcomes, proving that the right tools can unlock doors that once seemed firmly shut.

Another riveting example comes from a social media influencer who faced burnout from the pressures of constantly curating content. Seeking a fresh approach, they integrated AI-generated supermodels into their online presence. By using these digital personas to create engaging narratives and visually striking content, they not only alleviated their own workload but also captivated their audience in entirely new ways. As their follower count surged and brand partnerships flourished, they discovered a renewed passion for their work. This transformation underscores the potential of AI to rejuvenate careers and infuse innovation into the influencer landscape.

Entrepreneurs in the beauty industry have also experienced dramatic shifts thanks to AI supermodels. A makeup artist, once confined to local clientele, utilized AI-generated models to demonstrate their products on diverse digital faces. This strategy not only expanded their reach but also attracted collaborations with major beauty brands. Their success story showcases how the fusion of artistry and technology can amplify visibility and profitability, enabling even the most niche businesses to thrive in a competitive environment. With AI supermodels, the boundaries of creativity are pushed, empowering entrepreneurs to dream bigger and achieve more.

The inspiring stories of transformation through AI-generated supermodels are a testament to the power of innovation and adaptability. From fashion designers to influencers and beauty entrepreneurs, these individuals have embraced the digital revolution, leading to newfound success and fulfillment. As the landscape of social media continues to evolve, those willing to explore the potential of AI will undoubtedly find themselves at the forefront of a new era of entrepreneurship. The journey from obscurity to Insta-millionaire status is not just a possibility; it is an exhilarating reality waiting to be seized by the next wave of innovators.

Chapter 10: Your Journey to Becoming an Insta-Millionaire

Setting Your Goals and Vision

Setting your goals and vision is the first exhilarating step towards harnessing the power of AI-generated supermodels on social media. As you embark on this journey, it's crucial to define what success looks like for you. Are you aiming for brand partnerships, a booming online presence, or perhaps a revolutionary new business model that integrates AI technology with fashion? By clarifying your ambitions, you position yourself to create a roadmap that guides you through the myriad of opportunities available in this dynamic space. Let your imagination run wild as you envision the heights your venture could reach!

Once you have a clear picture of your goals, it's time to translate that vision into actionable steps. Break down your overarching ambitions into smaller, achievable milestones. This could involve launching your first AI-generated supermodel, creating engaging content that resonates with your audience, or mastering social media algorithms to maximize your reach. Each milestone you set should be specific, measurable, and time-bound, allowing you to track your progress and celebrate your successes along the way. Remember, every small victory brings you closer to your ultimate vision!

Your vision should not only focus on personal gain but also consider the impact you want to have on your audience and the industry as a whole. Think about how your AI-generated supermodels can challenge traditional beauty standards, promote inclusivity, or revolutionize marketing strategies. By aligning your goals with a greater purpose, you can create a brand that resonates deeply with your audience. This alignment can also enhance your credibility and attract like-minded partners who share your passion for innovation and social change.

As you navigate this thrilling landscape, be prepared to adapt and refine your goals as you learn from your experiences. The world of AI and social media is ever-evolving, and flexibility is key to staying ahead of the curve. Regularly revisit your vision and milestones, adjusting them based on feedback from your audience, changes in technology, or shifts in market trends. Embrace the journey as an opportunity for growth, allowing your vision to evolve in tandem with your understanding of the industry and your audience's desires.

Finally, surround yourself with a community that shares your enthusiasm and drive. Engage with fellow innovators, creators, and entrepreneurs who are also exploring the potential of AI-generated supermodels. This network can provide invaluable support, inspiration, and collaboration opportunities. By fostering connections with others who are equally passionate about this frontier, you amplify your chances of success. Together, you can push the boundaries of what's possible, turning your ambitious vision into a thriving reality in the exhilarating world of AI and social media.

Creating a Step-by-Step Action Plan

Creating a step-by-step action plan is crucial for anyone eager to harness the explosive potential of AI-generated supermodels on social media. The first step involves defining your goals. Are you looking to create a brand, drive traffic to your products, or build a network of followers? Clarity in your objectives not only sets the tone for your entire strategy but also helps in measuring success down the line. Write down your goals in a visually appealing format that inspires you every day. This will be the beacon guiding your journey through the exhilarating world of AI supermodels.

Next, dive into research and development. This is where the magic begins! Explore various AI tools and platforms that are available for generating supermodels. Familiarize yourself with the latest trends in AI technology, social media algorithms, and the types of content that resonate with your target audience. Utilize online courses, tutorials, and webinars to bolster your knowledge. The more you understand the landscape, the more equipped you'll be to navigate it effectively. Make a list of resources that can help you refine your skills, and don't hesitate to reach out to fellow creators for insights and collaboration opportunities.

Once you have a solid understanding of the landscape, it's time to brainstorm content ideas. Create a content calendar that outlines what you will post, when, and on which platforms. Your AI-generated supermodels should have engaging backstories, unique aesthetics, and captivating personalities that resonate with your audience. Experiment with different formats—photos, videos, stories, or live sessions—to see what generates the most engagement. This is the fun part where your creativity can truly shine! Don't shy away from being bold and experimental; sometimes, the most unexpected ideas can lead to viral success.

After mapping out your content strategy, focus on building your social media presence. Choose the platforms that align best with your target audience, whether it's Instagram, TikTok, or another emerging platform. Invest in high-quality visuals that showcase your AI supermodels in the best light. Interact with your audience through comments, polls, and direct messages to cultivate a community around your brand. Consistent engagement not only boosts your visibility but also fosters loyalty among your followers. Remember, social media is a two-way street; your audience will appreciate the effort you put into connecting with them.

Finally, measure and refine your strategy regularly. Use analytics tools to track engagement metrics, follower growth, and conversion rates. Analyze what works and what doesn't, and be willing to pivot your approach based on the data. Celebrate your wins, no matter how small, and learn from the setbacks. The journey to becoming an

Insta-Millionaire is filled with twists and turns, but with a well-structured action plan, you'll be well on your way to turning your dreams into reality. Embrace the adventure, stay enthusiastic, and let your passion for AI supermodels propel you forward!

Staying Motivated and Overcoming Challenges

Staying motivated in the fast-paced world of AI-generated supermodels is essential for anyone looking to capitalize on this exciting trend. The digital landscape is constantly evolving, and it can sometimes feel overwhelming. However, maintaining a positive mindset and focusing on your goals can propel you forward. Set clear, achievable milestones for your journey. Break your ambitions down into manageable tasks, and celebrate each small victory. This approach not only helps maintain motivation but also builds momentum that can carry you through tougher times.

Challenges are an inevitable part of any entrepreneurial journey, especially in a niche as dynamic as AI supermodels. You may encounter obstacles such as fluctuating trends, technical difficulties, or even competition from others in the field. Embrace these challenges as opportunities for growth. Each setback can teach you valuable lessons that refine your strategy and enhance your skills. Remember, every successful Insta-millionaire has faced their share of hurdles; it's how you respond that truly matters.

Surrounding yourself with a supportive community is another key factor in staying motivated. Connect with like-minded individuals who share your passion for AI supermodels and social media marketing. Engage in discussions, share insights, and collaborate on projects. This network can provide encouragement during tough times, and the exchange of ideas can spark creativity and innovation. Consider joining online forums, social media groups, or even local meetups where you can build these vital connections.

Furthermore, keep your vision clear and remind yourself why you embarked on this journey. Visualize your success regularly; envision yourself achieving your goals and reaping the rewards of your hard work. This mental imagery can serve as a powerful motivator, especially on challenging days when doubt creeps in. Create a vision board with images and quotes that inspire you, and place it in a spot where you'll see it daily. This tangible reminder of your aspirations will keep your enthusiasm burning bright.

Lastly, never underestimate the power of self-care in maintaining motivation. The hustle culture can sometimes lead to burnout, so it's crucial to prioritize your well-being. Schedule regular breaks, practice mindfulness, and engage in activities that rejuvenate your spirit. A clear and rested mind is far more effective in tackling challenges and seizing opportunities. By nurturing yourself, you'll be better equipped to navigate the exciting yet demanding world of AI-generated supermodels and emerge victorious in your quest for Insta-millionaire success.

www.ingramcontent.com/pod-product-compliance
Lightning Source LLC
Chambersburg PA
CBHW070137230526
45472CB00004B/1570